SEEKING
THE
PATH
TO LIFE

THEOLOGICAL MEDITATIONS
ON GOD
AND THE NATURE
OF PEOPLE,
LOVE, LIFE AND DEATH

Ira F. Stone

For People of All Faiths, All Backgrounds

JEWISH LIGHTS Publishing

Seeking the Path to Life: Theological Meditations On God And The Nature Of People, Love, Life And Death

© 1992 by Ira F. Stone

Library of Congress Cataloging in Publication Data
Stone, Ira F., 1949—
    Seeking the path to life: theological meditations on God and the nature of people, love, life and death / Ira F. Stone.
    p. cm.
ISBN 978-1-68336-284-5 (pbk)
ISBN 978-1-68336-285-2 (hc)

                                                            92-12090
                                                            CIP
1. Jewish meditations. 2. Judaism—Doctrines. I. Title.
BM724.S76 1993
296.3—dc20

First edition

Manufactured in the United States of America

Published by JEWISH LIGHTS Publishing

Dedicated to the memory of
Sam and Bessie Gruder, my grandparents,
for the lives they lived
and of
Hillel and Akiba Stone, my sons,
for the lives they could have lived.

CONTENTS

PREFACE

"**D**ead things come before Me and leave Me imbued with life." This rather curious statement attributed to God by the rabbis in the Midrash captures the movement of this book. I have experienced—and continue to experience—my life as a passage from death to life, with God as the agent of vital transformation. As a rabbi, I deal often with death. As a person, I've dealt with it more than I would like. This familiarity leads me to identify those times when my posture toward the world around me could only be described as being dead to life. Conversely my life has had more than its share of joy. At those moments, I feel "more alive" than I could have imagined possible.

These are not unique experiences. As I considered them more and more, especially in light of my almost instinctive attraction to the religious life, I came to understand that my sense of being alive was directly related to my strength at keeping myself open to God's Presence and that my sense of being dead was a blocking out of God.

It is out of this experience that I began to understand that the option "to choose life" that was put before the Jewish people in scripture was a daily task, even an hourly task. Amid responsibilities of earning a living, raising a family, maintaining a marriage, the choice was always before me: life or death—God's presence or God's absence.

The result of this realization (and my explanation of much of Jewish thought and practice in terms of it) is what follows. It is a description of a very personal coming to terms with life. It is my hope, however, that as personal as it may be, the reader will find the vying sensations of life and death familiar, also, in his or in her life. The meditations that follow are intended to act, in their own way, as certain forms of prayer have traditionally been intended to act: to focus our attention on the choice before us, to remind us of the possibility of overcoming those moments-of-death in our life which close us off from ourselves, from others and from God.

These meditations have performed that task for me and for congregants and friends with whom I've shared them. We have found that they can act as a preparation for prayer, a way of reminding oneself what is at stake in prayer. Or they can help facilitate reflection after prayer and extend the very opening up to life that liturgy ought to facilitate. While I speak here specifically of Jewish liturgy and Jewish prayer, worshippers in other traditions might find that the themes these meditations explore are transferable to their traditions as well.

It goes without saying that I write out of the spirit as experienced by a man. That the words I use may be overly weighted with masculine gender reflects the history of the English language. I am delighted that these linguistic habits are now changing. But using the still awkward solutions to some of the problems raised by gender in language, especially religious language, I believe would detain both writer and reader from reaching a more pressing destination. I have eliminated genderspecific references to human beings, but continue to use the masculine pronoun for God.

Drawing out what I hope is a coherent series of theological statements from the chaos and calm of my soul has been aided by many people over many years. Some of these people knew very well what they were doing. Others will be very surprised to find their names mentioned here.

To my wife, Annie, and to my children, Tamar, Yehoshua, and Shaul, I offer my deep gratitude for their having taught me the essential connection between theology and life. Sometimes against my will, they forced me to realize that the answers for which I had spent most of my life searching could only be extracted from the experience of learning to see each of them fully as persons and to accept and reciprocate their love.

Many others have given their support to this effort, and I offer my deepest thanks:

To my friends, Rabbi Dov Bard and Dr. Lane Gerber. In countless and, sometimes, endless conversations and correspondence they allowed me free rein in my speculations—always questioning and encouraging.

To my teacher, Rabbi Neil Gillman. Rabbi Gillman opened my eyes to what was possible. He took the issues with which I was grappling in isolation and affirmed their legitimacy in his own work. He read my statements critically, but compassionately. My work on these essays began under Rabbi Gillman's tutelage at a rabbinic retreat sponsored by the Jewish Theological Seminary of America. These retreats have enriched the lives and careers of American Conservative rabbis. I would like to express my appreciation to the seminary and its chancellor, Ismar Schorsch, and to the retreat program's coordinator, Rabbi Steven Shaw.

To my friends and former congregants at Congregation Beth Shalom in Seattle, Washington, who convinced me that ordinary people could not only take seriously in their lives the issues which obsessed me, but even thirsted for such discussion. I cannot thank them enough. And to my present friends and congregants at Temple Beth Zion-Beth Israel in Philadelphia, I extend my appreciation for their patience with a new rabbi simultaneously trying to learn how to serve them and to serve a quest that wouldn't wait.

I owe a great debt of thanks to Stuart Matlins and Jevin Eagle of Jewish Lights Publishing. Their enthusiasm for this project provided me with the confidence to see it through. Their support provided me with the conditions in which to do so. Arthur Magida, my editor, both taught me more about the craft of writing than I knew existed and insisted that what I wanted to say had to be clearly said or I might as well not say it. These were not always easy lessons to absorb, but Arthur was patient and the results convinced me of his wisdom. I am very grateful.

Finally, I want to thank Mrs. Phyllis Kramer, who typed, typed, and re-typed from my often indecipherable scrawl, all with constant good humor.

Above all, I praise and thank, glorify and extol, the Holy One of Israel who has allowed me to hear an echo of His Voice in my inadequate imagination. I have been truly blessed in my life and I pray that my efforts to extend His Voice through my work in the world have been pleasing to Him.

Into the shadow of my heart Your light
appears sometimes to enter,
sometimes trapped.

When I release my love, Your love
floods from me and back and I submit.

The hands of my lovers, my children,
my memories, reach over one another
toward You in me.

They discover me in You and together
they and You and I rise to meet each other.

1

FINDING THE WORDS

Silence was a big part of my growing up. While, since then, I have come to appreciate silence, for a little boy it meant loneliness. As a young boy wandering through the valley of loneliness, the music of the words of Torah and prayer became my companions.

I loved the synagogue service, although I did not understand the complex ideas of the liturgy. It was the music of those words, for reasons I do not entirely understand even now, that stirred something within me.

I did not come from a particularly religious home, but we were affiliated with a synagogue, celebrated the holidays, and observed the laws of mourning. I also received a minimal Jewish education. My grandfather, who was often silent, created a bond with me through that silence. This loving, inter-generational bond emanated from our shared experience of the synagogue service.

When I began to study the words of Torah and prayer many years later, I often experienced their meaning with an immediacy that required little or no verbal elaboration. Yet, when I entered the rabbinate and stood before a congregation or in a roomful of mourners or sat with a woman dying in my arms, silence, though sometimes helpful, was not sufficient. Questions required answers. Words had to be found to translate the music of the words of Torah, law, and prayer into more ordinary words. A system of notation needed to be found which, like the notes on a musical score, could translate not the meaning of these words, but the *experience* of the music of these words. Such notes would flow from my soul into the souls of those whose lives mine touched.

I have searched for these words. I'm sorry that I didn't have them to whisper to my friend who choked to death from emphysema in my arms or to offer the young wife whom I had to tell that her husband and the father of her two young daughters had drowned. For many years, I have carried the pain of having been with these people at such moments; for many years, I have carried the memory of my grandfather's silent bond. Now, I have found the words that can translate the music of my soul, composed by the experience of Torah and prayer, honed in loneliness comparable to theirs.

My search for words begins at that juncture between divine loneliness and human loneliness captured in the notion that we are created in the image and likeness of God. It begins where the struggle of God to express Himself corresponds to my struggle to express myself through the mysterious source of human expression, the imagination.

GOD

God is where I come from and where I'm going. At any point along this continuum, He alone can know me fully. Knowing me fully, He is able to love me.

What I know of God is that I am created in His image. That is the most profound religious statement I've ever encountered. Not for what it tells me about me, but for what it tells me about God. Since I create the world I live in through language, so must God. Since I can love and nurture, so must God. Since I am easily hurt or destructively angry so, too, God.

But God's characteristics are not bound by death and, therefore, are fundamentally different from those characteristics in me. There are moments when the qualities we identify as being feminine are essential to my sense of self. Then, God is She, comfortably and lovingly, for me.

My nature is often contradictory. I can be frustrated, vindictive, sometimes nihilistic, often afraid. I believe this applies to God as well, but He can always be available in love behind these states even as I can be, too. I believe that God fails me only when His being is constrained by His immortality. I, on the other hand, must ultimately be human, which means I must die. And death is the only place where I am alone.

REVELATION

Imagination is the bridge between God and humans. It is not the locus of fiction, but the locus of truth. God speaks to us through the imagination. Although the imagination uses various faculties to transmit God's message, speech—the faculty we have most in common with God—is the primary faculty of His revelation. Speech can transmit sense, feeling, and law. Every human being is capable of sensing God's voice in his or her imagination. But some, either by virtue of training or as an inexplicable gift of their nature, can sense the presence of this voice more strongly and can articulate it more clearly.

We call these people poets or prophets. They are blessed by God. They "report" the experience of God's word in their imaginations as verse, narrative, parable, story or law. These, in turn, excite the imaginations of their listeners, who over time, collectively shape and reshape these reports on the basis of both their imaginations and their experiences.

Revelation, then, is personal and communal, shaped by poetry and history. It is ongoing and never-ending. Being faithful to this revelation as it emerges over time means being able to travel toward God on the bridge between God and human beings. It is the path which brings us closest to God in this life. Its authority is affirmed by our having been created with imaginations capable of hearing it.

REDEMPTION

Sin and suffering, pain and loneliness are the result of God's necessary absence in that part of the human drama that is death: "In death there is no remembering thee" (Psalm 6). Death is not a once-and-for-all proposition. It is a daily tide in the human spirit which, at a certain point, overwhelms the individual and is final.

Revelation is the medium through which Torah, the antidote to death-in-life, is made known. The promise of Torah is that death-in-life can be conquered just as, ultimately, death itself can be conquered. Redemption is the victory of life over death, the onset of immortality, the absorption of human life into the divine life. The yearning for redemption is the primary religious impulse. From time immemorial, to conquer death has been *the* human dream.

For Jews, this impulse is encapsulated in the Eden story. The ever-present possibility of return to Eden—which is sensed even in our lives now lived in exile from Eden—is accomplished through ritual. Prayer, sacrifice, and the various rituals which impose order on our experience of the world (and culminate in the weekly Sabbath) rebuff death-as-sin. Thus, we taste the promise of redemption before its advent. Life is suffused with the meaning of redemption, the eradication of death, Torah's defeat of death-in-life, and, by bringing the promise of a Redeemer, of a divine intercession, the defeat of death itself.

TORAH

Revelation is interpersonal. It begins in the imagination of an individual. It is shaped by the experiences of that individual and the experiences of the people who form the audience for this revelation. It returns from the people to the prophet, helps to raise up other prophets, and, in turn, shapes not only the imagination of an individual but, also, of an entire people. It fosters a tradition that contains the records of God's voice as heard by individuals and by an entire people over time. This tradition becomes the source for learning the paths that the revelation has illuminated, the disciplines that have expressed it, the rituals that have enlivened it.

Revelation resonates with the authority of God's presence via imagination as well as the people's sacred history. It becomes the starting point for all further revelations, individual or communal, within a particular culture. It expresses the essential nature of a people and their relationship with God.

For the Jewish people, the ongoing record of revelation is Torah. It is the Jewish bridge between the people and God over the abyss of death which separates them. For this reason, our tradition talks of Torah as a "tree of life," as "a spring of living waters," as "eternal life planted in our midst." As our people continue to encounter God, we continue to learn paths that reduce the moments-of-death in our lives. We learn how our ancestors and our prophets imagined such paths to look. We evaluate their reports in the light of our experiences and our encounters with God in our imaginations. We strive to add to the possibilities for reducing death-in-life, not to subtract from them.

By this standard, we test the ongoing truth of Torah. As the rabbis taught: "That you should live by them; not die by them."

CREATION

That which passes away is created. That which is eternal is uncreated. Life in the world we know is part of creation since it passes away.

Creation is distinguished from the eternal by death. In the account in Genesis of the Creation, God forbids humans from eating from the Tree of Life lest they "become like us," that is, that humans become like the eternal beings and gain eternal life. Creation is purposeful since the creator has planted the seeds of immortality into mortal life. The revelation of Torah can so strengthen the immortal aspects of mortal life that God Himself will entirely overcome death for us.

Creation, then, presupposes redemption, which is itself made known by and experienced partially in revelation. Creation has a goal which is clear to God, however mysterious it is for us. Since we understand ourselves to be created in the image of God and we know from Genesis that we are meant not to be alone, we suspect that promulgating creation was divine loneliness. Faced with that same loneliness, we, by emulating God, also create. Our creations are spurred by the need to create order out of chaos. Our creation of order imitates God's love, which created the order of the universe. Human creation, therefore, gives rise to loving human relationships.

GOD IS ONE

Existence consists of only two components: the eternal and the created, the mortal and the immortal. Each is complex. The complexity of the mortal mirrors the complexity of the immortal. Each mortal face and every mortal thought approximates an immortal face and an immortal thought. In the mortal realm, the sum of these diverse faces and thoughts comprises the full, sole expression of a single creation. The sum of these faces and thoughts in the immortal realm constitutes the full, sole expression of a single God.

Some cultures express the complexity of both the mortal and the immortal by imagining a multiplicity of gods. This understanding of the universe can be profound and helpful in minimizing moments-of-death in life. But the Jewish people, among others, collectively imagined a single intelligence behind the vast multiplicity of that intelligence's expression. The Jewish imagination has apprehended the efforts of this single intelligence to bring order to the complexity of existence as the mysterious goal toward which all existence is moving, especially through creation, and the triumph over death. The immortal intelligence is analogous to the soul. It has neither beginning nor end and resides in the created universe, which is analogous to the human body. The work of the divine intelligence is to bring order to the immortal elements of the universe. Thus, its task is to bring order to itself. It created in love the world to speak to from its solitude. The work of mortal intelligence is to bring order to itself, to overcome death—the ultimate division between itself and its creator—and to live forever in the universe within that creator.

2

BRIDGING THE ABYSS

Few experiences which need to be expressed are predictable. As I translated the music of my religious experience into words, I also realized that I had not fully assimilated some into the music of my own soul. To translate them, I had to find them. Yet, I could find them only by attempting to translate them.

I had only been a rabbi for one year when I learned how difficult and dangerous this quest could be. We already had two young children when my wife, Annie, gave birth prematurely to twin boys, Hillel and Akiba. Akiba lived only a few days. He died in our arms. Hillel struggled for life. Annie and I, the center of an outpouring of community support, gave ourselves completely over to supporting Hillel every day—nearly every hour—in his battle for life. He grew and gained strength as the weeks passed. He had been born just after the High Holy Days. Now, he became our Hanukkah gift as we took him home on the last day of the festival after more than six weeks in intensive care. He died in our bed four nights later of Sudden Infant Death Syndrome.

Our lives to that point had been an example to our many young congregants of how to face adversity. But we had hardly accustomed ourselves to that role when it changed again and we became teachers of appropriate Jewish mourning ritual. Many people who had never seen the grandeur of sitting shiva and reciting Kaddish learned it from us. It was an important lesson in a community of young families in which I would preside over an eerie number of funerals for children in the following few years. But it was a teaching job whose toll on me I wouldn't acknowledge for a long time to come.

Ritual and community had comforted me. But they also distracted me from the opportunity to understand a new, discordant music. The loneliness which I had sought to banish by contemplating myself in the image and likeness of God had returned with a vengeance. I had stared at the pit into which I had placed my own sons and had seen nothing. Loneliness could no longer be explained away by simple invocation of God's Presence. It had to be accepted as an unalterable fact of life.

I did not immediately recognize the importance of doing this. However, while trying to find the words to translate the experiences of my soul, this discordant strain emerged and demanded to be translated also. I was haunted by the words of the Psalmist: "Though I walk through the valley of the shadow of death I will fear no evil for You are with me." Yet, I had sensed that moment when God is *not* with us: He is with us in the *valley* of the shadow of death, but not in *death itself.* I found this thought strangely comforting since it eventually opened up for me unexpected vistas of thought. This next group of meditations emerged from a long, sometimes tortured quest for solace for the emptiness of my sons' deaths.

MOMENTS-OF-DEATH IN LIFE: THE PROBLEM OF EVIL

Death is what distinguishes the mortal from the immortal, the divine from the human. In every place and at every moment, God is present. We are never alone, except at the moment of death.

God cannot experience the fullness of our mortality. Since death is the absence of God, humans encounter it whenever they remove themselves from the presence of God. Whether because of greed or pride, or whether in conscious rebellion against God's presence, or in the false belief that we can ultimately prevail over mortality alone and live forever: Whatever the reason, sin is the act of punctuating life with God's absence, with death. It is the act of inserting death into life.

Evil is the accumulation of these moments-of-death in life. Evil, being death, is neither from God nor under His control. Death separates us from God but it is neither our creation nor God's. It is a consequence solely of our mortality.

Eradicating evil can only be accomplished by eradicating death, which can partially occur by reducing moments of God's absence in our lives. We do this through Torah, which is God's presence. To the extent that we keep His presence with us by clinging to Torah, we can minimize our participation in spreading death and sin. But fully eradicating death presupposes the end of our mortality. We must die. Only a miracle outside the mortal order—the resurrection of the dead and the gift of immortality—eliminates evil entirely, and establishes righteousness eternally.

THE MESSIAH AND THE RESURRECTION OF THE DEAD

If our mortality cannot be transcended, it has no meaning. If life after death is the goal of life, why not hasten death's arrival through suicide? Yet, the certain existence of life beyond death lends ultimate meaning to this worldly life.

How can this be? We must understand that this life and the next are continuous. In this life, we have all of the elements of life in the messianic world—except for immortality. That is, we are tempted by sin and tempted to sin. By tuning our imagination to hear the voice of God, we discover how to increase God's presence in our midst and, thereby, how to reduce the death which is sin.

Thus, this world and the messianic world are not far apart. But as close as they are, the gulf between them is profound. To bridge this gap we pray for a Messiah, for one so blessed that no death is possible in his life. He will be so righteous that though he is mortal, there will be no absence of God's presence, even for a moment, in his life.

The effect of someone who so fully exemplifies creation's potential will be dramatic. The mysterious goal of creation will finally be fulfilled. The time will be at hand for God to remove the final barrier between this world and redemption—the barrier of death. Since we believe that except for death, this world and the redeemed world are continuous, and since we believe that our every organ and faculty is imperfect only because it withers and dies and that, otherwise, it fully imitates God, we can understand why Jewish tradition says we will be resurrected as fully *embodied* spiritual beings. We do not now know ourselves as only creatures of the spirit or of the body, but we know ourselves as whole beings consisting inseparably of both manifestations. As we are now, so we will be at redemption. As we have a place now, so, too, we will have a place then. But, by ultimately living without death, we will also live without sin, as each of us perfects our imaginations to hear the voice of God in its fullness.

EXILE

Exile is living with the weight of the full knowledge of one's mortality. Traditionally, this knowledge entered the world in the Garden of Eden. It is a common misconception that our exile from the Garden ushered death into human life. Nothing in the story indicates that we were immortal before expulsion. In chapter 3 of Genesis, when God cursed the ground because of Adam's actions, He also cursed Adam and his descendants. Adam would eat of the ground's produce in sorrow, be plagued by thorns and thistles, take bread from the ground by the sweat of his brow until he returned to the ground from which he had been taken: "For dust thou art and unto dust will thou return."

Man knew that he had been created, and he had participated in the creation of Woman. Their origin in dust had always implied that they would end in dust. Yet, they were not aware of their fate until they were exiled. Their sorrow and their labor make sense only in light of human mortality. Man and woman's origins in dust and return to dust did not depend on their having been cursed. It depended on their mortality. Furthermore, in Genesis 3:23, God said that by eating from the tree of Good and Evil, humans had attempted to usurp the power of God. Exile followed after God concluded that people might now attempt to achieve immortality by eating from the Tree of Life.

Adam and Eve became aware of their mortality by fleeing from the presence of God for just an instant. Experiencing a moment-of-death led to the knowledge of death.

If exile followed paradise in Genesis, it also followed the failure to acknowledge God's redeeming power in Exodus. For the people of Israel who were in bondage, which is as far as one can get from God, life was predominantly moments-of-death. But the further the slave was from God, the more powerful was his cry to God. In Exodus, a model for redemption appears in the most powerful encounter with God in the Jewish imagination —that of God and Moses. Moses' absence from God's presence was minimal. His ability to meet God at will was revolutionary and precipitated the first redemption of the Jewish people. The people Israel, freed from Egypt, were bound for redeemed life in the land of Israel. But a people of bondage, a people who were thoroughly suffused with death-in-life and who had no way to supplant moments-of-death with moments-of-life, were not prepared for redemption. That required the life-giving revelation of Torah.

Thus, the events at Sinai were a necessary step between bondage and redemption. Yet even armed with Torah, the death consciousness was so strong that the people succumbed to it and could not accept the reality of their encounters with God in their collective imagination. Their faithlessness made their redemption falter until it was replaced by exile. In the continuing presence of death-in-life, and in the persistence of faithlessness, exile continues today.

FAITH AND FAITHFULNESS

Faith and faithfulness are essential for achieving the full potential of every moment in life, for drawing life—not death—out of a moment. Faith is the ability to believe that what happens in one's imagination and in one's people's imagination is truth, not fiction. It requires courage to withstand the blandishments of a culture which equates faith with ignorance and that insists on opposing imagination to truth. Faithfulness is the ability to live by the light of whatever one's faith has discovered. Together, faith and faithfulness provide the environment in which choosing moments-of-life over moments-of-death in life can flourish.

Our faith in the reality of revelation and our faithfulness to its evolving content provides the comforting ability to make order of the chaos of life. It is this order which provides the setting for holiness, for God's presence.

Like all human attributes, faith and faithfulness are also attributes of God. For God must also respect both the medium of revelation and the content of the revelation in which He participates. That God is faithful to His creation and to the various revelations of Himself is the first principle of faith itself: our ability and our courage to believe in God's faithfulness. God's faithfulness has not only been demonstrated in the prophetic imagination, but has also continually been experienced by our people in their history. That He is with us in love and that He is faithful to His word emerges from that word itself as well as from our historic experience as a people. To this day, the survival of our people's prophetic imagination is a testament to our faith and to God's faith, to our faithfulness and to God's faithfulness.

COVENANT

As separate as God and people are from one another, we do not only communicate with each other, we also act in the world with each other. The mutually binding agreement to act together is called covenant. The terms of the covenant are communicated via the voice of God as apprehended in the collective imagination of a people and shaped by the historic experience of a people.

God makes covenants with every people, appropriate to their collective imagination and their history. His covenant with Israel is an example of such covenants. The choice of Israel as the model for His way of making covenants is mysterious. But in the very mystery of this choice, the model is at work. For we learn, for example, from the story of Abraham that the covenant depends on the ability of a prophet to hear it and to convincingly convey it to his people.

Not all peoples have yet had such a prophet nor heard and affirmed God's offer of a covenant. While the terms of each covenant will be constantly reshaped by imagination tempered by history, the eternity of each is assured. God does not break faith with the Jewish people nor with any other people with whom He has made a covenant. Each covenant is a token of His faithfulness. The suggestion that any one of them is transitory demeans God and the nature of His covenants. Part of the evolving understanding of the terms of the covenant is that each covenanted people must fully acknowledge the truth of His covenants with other peoples.

HOLINESS

That which is entirely separate from us and beyond the reach of death is termed holy. Essentially, holiness is separateness. By extension, distinguishing between that which brings moments-of-death in life and that which militates against such moments also distinguishes between the holy and the profane.

In limiting the moments-of-death in life, we experience the growing presence of God in our lives. Sensing this presence and acknowledging it is also, by further extension, holiness. One who continually separates himself from moments-of-death in life is a holy person. A people who together devise disciplines by which they respond to the voice of God as apprehended in their imagination, rituals which limit moments-of-death in life, can be called a holy people. A land which the imaginative experience of a people considers indispensable to their striving to minimize moments-of-death in life can be a holy land. Rituals and customs which assist in this process can be called holy.

Stories and songs, foods and clothing, all the arts and sciences of the world can be either holy or profane. Those which assist in conquering moments-of-death are holy. Those which remove us from that presence are profane.

ISRAEL

The land of Israel is holy. Holiness is the quality of being filled with the presence of God and of having that presence acknowledged by the inhabitants of the land.

God's presence floods every land. In many, His presence is acknowledged. Given each people's covenant with God, each may possess a holy land. While responsibility for maintaining the holiness of the land depends upon its people, the land remains forever intrinsically holy. It functions as a reminder of an ideal toward which the people must aim.

The people, Israel, and the land of Israel are inextricable in the imagination from which God's voice emanates. For a Jew, to live in the Holy Land and to recognize the holiness of the land is the ideal religious condition. Neither living in the land and disregarding its holiness nor living piously outside of the land are sufficient for achieving this ideal religious condition. For this reason, both the land and the people are called "Israel."

The people, Israel, is also holy. Holiness is being filled with and acknowledging the presence of God. Every people may be a holy people since the presence of God fills their lives. The people, Israel, has acknowledged and welcomed and valued that aspect of God which is present in each of its members.

Living in the land, we must recognize its holiness. The legitimacy of living outside the land is judged by our acting on behalf of the land. For a Jew, neither living with the community of Israel while disregarding its holiness nor living piously in isolation from the people Israel is sufficient for achieving this condition.

The Jew and the Jewish community are inextricable. The land and the people are one. Since achieving this double oneness allows for the fullest arena for minimizing the absence of God's presence, it is also a prerequisite for the advent of the Messiah.

3

THE WAY OF RENEWAL

L *ife Is With People.* This is the title of a book I read early in my coming to choose a Jewish life for myself. Its description of European Jewish life in the *shtetl* before the First World War was reinforced for me a few years later when I read Abraham Joshua Heschel's *The Earth Is The Lord's*, a description of the deep spirituality of this same community. Both books kindled a deep emotional response in me. Everyone around me was rushing to meet the twenty-first century while I was longing to meet the nineteenth, or the twelfth, or even the first. To do this, I had to learn two languages: Hebrew and Aramaic. I had to fit my life into new rhythms. I fled the New York of my youth and its complacent Judaisms and discovered—with surprising gratification— that I was not the only second- and third-generation American Jew living in Santa Barbara concerned with meeting the past.

Long before I considered becoming a rabbi, I had to struggle to become a Jew. During the course of that struggle, I had learned patience. I had learned that the power of liturgy and ritual release themselves as needed into one's life in spurts. After I had become a rabbi and was faced with the emptiness of the death of my sons, the liturgy and the rituals of my new life led me to the other side of the abyss, to the possibilities of renewal that I now recognize as their true goal. In the first days of shiva, I had surrounded myself with a shell. I could go through the motions, but could not connect with those around me. I, who thought he already knew how to pray, learned to pray again. I, who thought he already knew how to study, learned to study again. It was this sense of the imperative of renewal, the opacity of all life itself, that brought me back to people.

Renewal gives meaning to every phase of life. Jewish renewal is grounded in communal energy. Longing for the past, I realized, had not been a case of mere nostalgia. Nor did it preclude welcoming the future. Rather, it was an instinctive desire to be part of an ever-renewing community; to be carried along to self-discovery by people who were constantly discovering themselves. It engendered the desire in me to help that community, whose catastrophes made my personal tragedies pale by comparison, awaken to the powers of renewal carried in its history and its poetry.

PRAYER

The link between God and human beings is language. Language is multidimensional. It can convey, simultaneously the voice of God and our response, as well as our voices and God's response. Prayer is that dimension of language which begins in the human heart and carries that voice through the imagination to God. Ideal prayer returns to the human heart from the responsive heart of God.

In Jewish tradition, we imagine such a responsive movement between God and angels proceeding eternally as the ideal toward which human prayer strives. Since the only distinction between angels and humans is death, without death we would proclaim God's glory continually. Our mortality limits our ability to do so. The fewer moments-of-death in life we experience, the greater our ability to pray. We may pray for forgiveness, but we cannot pray in the absence of God.

Our response to God in prayer may be spontaneous, and this is laudatory. But often we attribute our situation as human beings not to the quality of our relationship to God, but to our own power. We take the credit for our successes and assume blame for our failures. Often, the pace or the sheer noise of contemporary life cause us to ignore the possibility of a response to God. Fixed prayer lets us be called into the presence of God against the grain of our mortality. Traditional liturgy lets us lift up in our imagination not just the words of our ancestors, but also their very merit and their relation with the Divine. Since the words of prayer are, in their way, prophecy, we join through them with God himself. Prayer is the doorway to the level of prophecy for those of us not yet able to reach such a level otherwise.

STUDY AS WORSHIP

God and people have reason in common. The distinction between us and other creatures is reason. Reason is not limited to the intellect. It also includes the ability to reflect on the experiences of all the emotions. A human being can stand back and reflect upon whatever proceeds from the mind. It is this ability to reflect which constitutes imagination.

The link between our imagination and God is language. The voice of God heard in imagination is prophecy. Only those specially gifted or those trained over many years can hear God's voice in prophecy. But the ability to participate in the divine-human dialogue is open to all through prayer and study. In study we direct the force of intellect and emotional reflection onto the collected record of the prophetic encounter with the voice of God. Through study, we concentrate our reason in an effort to meet God. We are lifted out of mortality by attending to that part of ourself which must be immortal since we share it with God. Every attempt to be lifted beyond mortality—to transcend the created—is called worship.

DEEDS OF LOVING KINDNESS

God's presence in humanity is not limited to one person but resides equally in each person and awaits acknowledgment by that person. The failure of one person to acknowledge God's presence at any moment means that God's presence in the entire world is diminished by exactly the amount of that disbelief. No one but the Messiah can ever be able to avoid such moments, but the task of each of us is to try.

Torah prescribes a way which allows each of the people of Israel to make God's presence palpable. We have seen that study and prayer constitute two parts of this way. The third consists of deeds of loving kindness.

We recognize God's presence in the lives and faces of other humans. And we respond to that presence by trying to nurture it in the lives of others. To feed the hungry, clothe the naked, heal the sick, or comfort the bereaved is to emulate God's relationship with humanity and to extend, as it were, the reach of God's love and, therefore, His presence. At the same time, by helping to free others from the oppression of their afflictions, we also help them to more successfully maintain God's presence in their lives. And we demonstrate that the way of God— a way of peace and a way of wholeness—has consequences in our lives. Such a demonstration inspires those who have received help and those who have witnessed our deeds of love and compassion.

SACRIFICE*

Sacrifice was the highest form of worship in the Bible and was treated as such by subsequent Jewish commentators. Taking seriously the importance of this form of worship in the Bible and, more importantly, its centrality in the discussions of the rabbis of the first centuries of the common era, requires that we suspend contemporary distaste for actual animal sacrifice and discover the theology which sustained this institution and made remembering it so important in Jewish liturgy long after the Temple in Jerusalem had ceased to exist.

In sacrifice we could, for a fleeting moment, imagine our own death and, yet, go on living. No other form of worship can bring a person so near to the prospect of death. Therefore, no other form of worship can so effectively liberate a person from the fear of living in the shadow of death.

Worshippers came to the Temple to dispel their terror of death's solitude by conjuring a moment in which they shared the experience of death with God. But strictly speaking, death shared with God is no longer death, for there is no death in God. The experience of death which is no longer death sustains for the worshipper the promise of immortal life.

The cessation of this ritual after the destruction of the Temple necessarily precipitated a spiritual crisis of enormous proportion. The elaborate re-enactment of sacrificial rites introduced by the rabbis of the Mishnah was intended to provide an avenue for drawing near to God. The Hebrew word for "sacrifice," *korban*, is taken from the Hebrew word meaning "to draw near." Reciting passages from the Bible, the Mishnah, and the Talmud that contain the laws of the sacrifices, intoning Sabbath and Festival prayers that describe the sacrificial offerings, and saying the blessing petitioning God to restore the Temple that is in the daily *Amidah* prayer all illustrate the rabbinic teaching: "'After the destruction of the Temple,' God said to Abraham, 'your children shall study the laws concerning sacrifices and I will consider it as though they had actually offered them, and I will forgive their sins'"(Talmud Megilah 31b). The need to maintain the theology of sacrifice overcame the impossibility of performing them.

In an even deeper way, sacrifice answered other equally important questions: What is the nature of my relationship with others? Does my definition of myself include or exclude others? Is my ego the sum of myself?

Daily we confront these questions, consciously or not: "I want this." "I want that." "You should serve me."

These statements all presuppose an answer to the question of our relationship to other people. Sacrifice forced us to share. In the act of sacrifice the worshipper shared the enjoyment of the fruits of the world with God and with the priests, representing the community. Some sacrifices were left on the altar, some eaten by the priests, some by the worshippers. It forced us to recognize that what we possess is only partly ours. We imaginatively shared with God our good fortune and our sins, our desires and our satisfactions, depending upon the sacrifice called for. All that we meant by "ours" included God.

Sacrifice also called on us to include our community in our understanding of what constituted our "selves." Solitude was considered a stage in the development of our personality. As children, we learned how to separate ourselves from the world around us, but as mature adults our sense of self required the inclusion of others.

In place of the actual Temple, rabbinic Judaism produced a Temple out of the rhythms of life. Study, prayer and deeds of loving kindness, all performed within the cycle of festivals and Sabbaths, replaced the offering. The rabbinic system of living "as though" sacrifice could be offered by words and deeds provides a way of vicariously achieving the goals which sacrifice had sought. To the extent that the rituals are performed with attention to their connection both to the question of life and death and to the question of our relationship to others, they remain at the core of Jewish living.

* Portions of this essay previously appeared incorporated into my article: "Korbanot: Recovering Our Spiritual Vocabulary" in *Judaism* 40, No. 1 (Winter 1991): 52—59.

DANGER AND SAFETY

The traditional imagination of the Jewish people perceived certain natural events as indications of an intersection between the divine and the mortal. Since the divine and the mortal are unable to fill the same space, since they are separated by death, precautions had to be taken to protect humans from the presence of death. There is no analogue in contemporary thought to the concept of danger, *tumah*, and safety, *tahara*, which the tradition devised. Even in contemporary Jewish practice this concept has all but disappeared, though some remnants of it survive. The use of the *mikva*, ritual immersion, by women after their menstrual period, the washing of hands before eating and before prayer, and a few other practices remain.

Understanding the system of *tumah* and *tahara* is, however, still important in that a large amount of Jewish theological energy was once invested in it. Also, its concern with the moments-of-death which are present in life recommends it as a source of meditation from which new ideas for grappling with this still significant problem may emerge.

At every point at which human beings and God meet, the death which separates them is palpably present. There is a danger in these encounters that we could come too close to the line that separates us, to the mystery of death.

Encounters in life between the mortal and the immortal fall into several broad categories. Traditionally, they include moments when we are in the presence of death. Also when leprosy, seminal flow, or menstrual blood occur because these were times when the individual was assumed to have veered too close to the divide between the known and the unknown, between the living and the dead. The person who had become *tame*, "endangered," had to undergo rituals of separation from the community and immersion in a ritual bath. Once restored to the level of fitness required to perform rituals, he or she had to bring a sacrifice to the Temple. It was at the Temple itself that the laws of danger and safety were most stringently enforced. For it was at the Temple that the ceremonies of life and death, the drawing close of humans and God, were centered.

With the destruction of the Temple, the rabbis extended the notion of the need for safety in the face of danger to the institutions which replaced sacrifice. Study, prayer, and meals as sacred occasions occur amid the priestly laws of ritual fitness because they are widely understood as the ground upon which we encounter God in the post-Temple world. Similarly, these rituals have been preserved for those situations where they are clearly still appropriate, such as moments when death is actually encountered. Such rituals include washing of the deceased before burial and washing of the hands after leaving the cemetery.

I would suggest that far from obviating the need for attention to *tahara*, our contemporary world requires even greater diligence regarding such safety. As Judaism has expanded the opportunities for our drawing close to God, not only in prayer and study but in good works, in loving relationships, in sexuality, in childbirth and child rearing, contemporary Jews should try to expand the areas in which they are conscious of their proximity to the line that divides them from death. They should be as respectful toward it as were our ancestors. Living in the twentieth century, a century in which the depersonalization of death threatens to numb us to its reality, reinvigorating the Jewish concern with the mystery and terror of death's presence calls not for discontinuation of the rituals of *tahara* but for their extension wherever possible.

4

LIVING IN THIS LIFE

Living life after suffering the utter solitude of accompanying a loved one to the grave and then creating a new life which takes that lonely experience seriously requires that the way one lives with people change. Renewing and invigorating life comes only from being with people—not from retreating to the solitude of pain and despair.

This has been the most difficult part of my own journey. Prayer and study are easy. Loving is not. Confronting anger is not. Living with sadness is not. Moreover, just learning how difficult these things are almost inevitably heaps pain and hurt on those whose love one is seeking. Such has been my experience. The death of my infant sons, Hillel and Akiba, only exacerbated my tendency to withdraw from emotional encounter. After the shock of the abandonment caused by death, I insulated myself against further abandonment. I regret the pain this caused my wife and children. I am grateful that their prodding helped me to begin to learn that I was fleeing what I most needed.

I am also grateful to my experience in psychotherapy. I came to therapy highly suspicious, and I still believe that it rests on a truncated vision of human personality: it does not take seriously enough our need to submit before God. But despite these philosophic qualms, I found a gifted healer who nurtured those parts of my psyche whose very existence she may have doubted. Her acceptance of my pain and my fears (as well as her acceptance of my strengths and my talents) was vitally important to my attempt to discover these words. With her help, I began to trust my impulse to discover life after the experience of death. With her encouragement, I discovered the way moments-of-death in life clouded my relationships with others.

Thus I came again to God. And from God, I came to understand that the way to God was through people. I came to understand, also, that the way to God began with those people closest to me who were willing to love me, and whom I have only begun to allow myself to love.

LOVE

Love is the state of being passionately engaged with a separate personality in its entirety and being loved is allowing that separate personality to be passionately engaged with one's self. It is characterized by a desire to nurture the other unconditionally as well as a desire to be nurtured by the other.

Only God is capable of perfect love. At no time is God's love unavailable to us, though it may be hidden by other qualities, such as God's anger. Our love of God, as well as the love of one person for another, is imperfect to the degree that we are alone in moments-of-death. At such times, our deeply rooted lonesomeness precludes the possibility of being engaged with others, whether divine or human.

There is no love in death or in moments-of-death in life. Instead, we convince ourselves that the other is also dead, and we act in anger at our abandonment. Human love—as well as God's love—merely washes over us in the hope that it may find a crack through which to enter our shell, and, by so doing, begin to dispel our isolation by nurturing and accepting us. Thus, to the extent that we seek ways to eliminate God's absence, His love finds us and bathes us in its glory.

The full power of God's love lets us accept and return His love. In so doing, we again learn to accept and reciprocate the love of others.

SEXUALITY I

We are created in the image of God. This is a fundamental statement of Jewish faith. What we know most about God is embedded in this statement. Moreover, the very fact that we are created at all teaches us that the act of creation is one of the primary attributes of God, if not *the* primary attribute. From this, we learn that creating life is also one of the primary attributes, if not *the* primary attribute of human beings.

In the Torah's description of creation, life emerged when God imposed order on the chaos of the universe with His love and when He decided to nurture and sustain His creation. Similarly, out of the chaos of human passion, we are provided with the possibility of bringing forth new life.

Sexuality is the human counterpart of divine creation. Just as God created out of the passionate engagement of His love, so, too, do human beings create life out of the passionate engagement of their love. Just as God took responsibility for nurturing and sustaining His creation, so, too, must human beings take responsibility for nurturing and sustaining their creation. And just as God created by allowing space for mortality, so, too, human beings know that their creation will die. Having the knowledge of faith in a life beyond creation, the very act of procreation itself becomes an affirmation of the promise of redemption.

SEXUALITY II

If male or female are created in the image of God, God's image must include both masculine and feminine elements. Separating these elements into human men and women divides one divine attribute. Since the urge to recombine undergirds the sexual impulse, the Torah records God saying at the creation of human beings: "It is not good for man to be alone."

Drawing together these divine elements is, therefore, not limited to the virtue of procreation, since it fulfills the divine imperative against loneliness. Human sexuality, then, responds both to the drive to create and to the drive against loneliness. In this second response, sexual activity is not limited to procreation. Rather, it is grounded in the joy of physically coming together.

Our experience in the world teaches us that every man retains traces of the female and every woman retains traces of the male. It is also clear that attraction between members of the same sex is possible and natural when these male and female elements are distributed with sufficient inequality Mortality itself implies the presence of myriad inequalities in human nature and its attempt to emulate God. These inequalities cannot be predicted and are part of the nature of creation. No one inequality is morally more or less unequal.

Therefore, a loving attraction between people of the same sex that struggles against moments-of-death in life, and against the absence of God that is sin, is a response to the need to combine the male and female elements of divinity in those created beings. What the Torah calls an "abomination" applies to sex occurring between members of the same gender in whom these divine male and female elements are *not* distributed unequally, that is those who are not innately drawn to members of the same sex, but are only engaging in an arbitrary act of gratification. This interpretation likewise condemns those encounters in which the passionate engagement of love is not present, which is lust.

The absence of love in heterosexual relationships is also lust which, by debasing a divine attribute, constitutes a moment-of-death in life.

WOMEN

Revelation is the ongoing process in which the voice of God is encountered in the imagination, shaped by our people's experience of history and tested by its ability to help minimize moments-of-death in life.

This process cannot cease even for single moment. The voice of God sounds eternally; some human being is eternally striving to hear it and history is continually shaping it. By this process, God's word sustains the world and moves it closer to redemption.

The clearest example in contemporary Judaism of the working of this revelatory process appears in recent changes of traditional attitudes toward women and their spiritual life. That men and women have different natures and roles is a given in our tradition. That those differences should not—and were not—intended to denigrate women is clear from the opening verses of the Torah: "Male and female, He created them." However, the traditional roles of men and women, appropriate as they may have been (and to some extent still are), clearly contributed to the denigration of women's spiritual potential as we entered the present era. Historic experience opened the imagination of men and women to hear a new word of God. The process of testing the content of that word, of shaping it into human law, poetry song, and other works of human-divine interaction is unfolding before our eyes.

This is an exciting, if somewhat troubling experience, as new roles for men and women emerge even as the primordial differences between the sexes remain. And since the voice of God is, as always, muffled, we require the experience of history and trial-and-error as we stumble along this road. In this, as in every revelation, our criteria for truth generates moments-of-life to replace the moments-of-death in life contained in every act of degradation.

ANGER

Anger results from our inability to admit the disparity between what we want and what is. It is a consequence of the impossibility of perfection in the created world in which the *idea* of perfection nevertheless exists. It is, therefore, grounded in the distance between the mortal and the immortal.

Anger generates great energy in both humans and God. God's anger results from the disparity between what He wants for us and what we are.

The energy generated by anger can be either constructive or destructive. When it reduces the moments-of-death in life, it is positive. When it causes us to be further removed from the presence of God, it is negative. In such stories as the destruction of Sodom and Gemorrah, the bringing of the flood, or the scattering of the builders of the Tower of Babel, God's anger and the energy it generates are models for acting on our anger and its energy. Typically, God's anger is ignited by injustice, by deceit, by cruelty and by unfaithfulness. He directs the energy generated by this anger at combating the causes of these conditions. God's anger can reestablish the equilibrium of the world. It aims to eliminate moments-of-death in life. It is life-giving.

But these biblical stories also tell of God's anger being potentially destructive. This destructive energy causes God to withdraw His presence from humanity or to contemplate such withdrawal. In these instances, we learn that we can attempt to dissuade God from acting on His anger. Abraham, Moses, and other prophets remind God of human imperfection and of God's own promise to maintain the life of this creation by His presence.

Human beings also typically become angry when confronted with injustice, deceit, cruelty and faithlessness. The responses characteristic of God when He is angry—life-giving or destructive—are also common to humans.

Following the example of the prophets, each of us has a mandate to assuage the destructive energy of anger in ourselves, in other people, and in

God. We also have a mandate to accept the life-giving energy that emerges from the anger that is constructively channeled, whether it comes from God or people.

SADNESS

Sadness is either the profound sense that one is not loved or that someone about whom one cares feels that he or she is not loved. This feeling may cause us to feel either as though another perceives us as if we were "dead," or that we cannot perceive the other as fully alive. In either case, this inability to connect in intimacy results in sadness. Sadness, in turn, isolates the person experiencing it from others. It may multiply itself until the individual is so far from the sense of life that results from otherwise being in the presence of God that he or she appears all but physically dead.

We are also sad when we imagine that we are severed from the love of God. This can only occur at moments-of-death, since God cannot enter these. Usually, we are angry at being abandoned in death or in moments-of-death. We project that death onto God's love, and refuse that love when it is offered. We are then further isolated and more profoundly saddened.

The antidote to sadness is to experience the intimacy that is love. To allow oneself to be nurtured is to accept one's own vulnerability before both God and human beings. Allowing God to nurture us breaks the isolation and sense of abandonment that is death or death-in-life.

When intimacy, acceptance and nurture replace isolation, deceit and rejection, then love replaces sadness.

GOD'S HEALING POWER

Three times a day the faithful Jew prays for healing. Does God heal the sick? How? Why do some who are ill recover and others do not? Does God heal both the body and the spirit—or only the body or the spirit? These questions must occur to anyone who says at morning, at noon, and at night, "Blessed art Thou O Lord, He who heals the sick amongst your people Israel."

These questions, in fact, must occur even to those who do not so pray.

But there are other questions that should be asked even before these: What is illness? Why does it exist? Is it, as some say, a punishment? If so, are all those who suffer illness less righteous than more healthy people? Or, as others say, is illness amoral, outside the power of God to influence, a matter of pure physical action and reaction?

What is health? What is healing? When we pray for healing are we praying that God will grant the wisdom to human healers to be able to discover and to treat what ails us?

We use the term "health" to describe our movement along the continuum from life to death. Such movement is inevitable. It is a consequence of our mortality. But, more properly, health also describes our ability to choose moments-of-life and not moments-of-death in life, given our present place on this life-death continuum. Health describes both the state of our inevitable physical deterioration and the consequences of that deterioration on our spiritual life. To pray for healing is to pray for an enhanced ability to choose moments-of-life over moments-of-death in life that are commensurate with our physical state.

JOY

Joy is the experience of well-being that comes with love that is properly received. It is the opposite of sadness; the goal of repentance; the context for atonement. It is experiencing life in such a way that neither the flight from death nor the inevitability of death inhibits us. Rather, we feel fully imbued with the sense of immortality which we know will finally be ours in the life of the world to come. Joy is a foretaste of that world in this world.

The goal of religious life is to enable us, in this world, to taste the joy of the world to come as fully as possible, and to punctuate this world's inevitable pain and death with moments of the joy of the next world. Since joy depends on love, one can only know joy in relation to another. Both the other and the self must be capable of that passionate engagement which recognizes each as fully alive.

Since joy is the taste of a world without death, it is a taste of that mode of being in which we and God are in perfect relationship with one another. This perfection of the divine-human relationship implies our ability to love God fully and to be fully alive to Him. And, in return, to accept unconditionally God's love of us and His will that we fully choose life and fully choose His presence.

WAR

War is the opposite of sacrifice. It is the victory of death-in-life as opposed to the possibility of life without death. It is the appropriation of death by human beings, who take it from God and hoard it. It is the collective aggrandizement of the mortal over the immortal.

War is inevitable in the course of human affairs. As a manifestation of death-in-life, war is no less a legitimate part of the human drama than sin, suffering, pain, and loneliness. War against evil can be used to justify combat because extreme evil is the extreme absence of God. But, in fact, the extreme absence of God is the extreme presence of death. And the extreme presence of death is war.

Evil breeds war. And like an illness that must run its course, evil will lead to war. Those who consider themselves good and who use war to combat evil are actually the agents of evil. They are inevitably drawn into evil's need for war. Thus, war is never good, and it is always potentially avoidable through repentance. Those who consider themselves good can fight evil with their own penitent lives, while those in whom evil is rampant can avoid war by their repentance. Without such repentance, war follows.

THE NATURAL WORLD

In its continuous unfolding, the natural world is the context within which life proceeds. As death separates us from God, it also emphasizes those aspects of our humanity which separate us from nature. Nature embodies a process of death and rebirth that gives it the appearance of being actually deathless: it symbolizes the immortal. The experience of death ends our experience of ourselves, of our consciousness. Because of this, we alone are fully mortal.

As a symbol of the immortal in this world, nature, like God, can provide moments-of-life without death for people to reflect upon. The depth of our response to the beauty of a natural scene or the peace experienced by our sense of nature's order helps to anchor us in a larger frame of reference for our lives. Just as we can deny the presence of God by expanding the moments-of-death in our lives, so, too, we can deny the life-affirming potential of nature by expanding the moments-of-death in life in relation to it.

Denying God's presence, as we have seen, can bring punishment. Debasing nature can also bring punishment: pollution, resource depletion, epidemic, and political instability. In fact, according to the prophets of Israel, nature can punish us both for sins against itself and for sins against other manifestations of the immortal.

We have spoken of human beings as fully embodied spirits in this world who will remain fully embodied spirits in the messianic world. We have said that we and God are bound together by a covenant, and that Torah is the covenantal relationship of the spirit. The relationship between us and the divine is also expressed in a covenant between ourselves and nature. God calls upon us to maintain and sanctify nature just as we maintain and sanctify Torah. If we do this, nature will maintain and nourish us. But until now we have brought a flood of death against nature and are threatened with being severed from its sustenance. Repentance is required.

5

LIVING BEYOND THIS LIFE

Being conscious of death, committed to people, and faithful to a future that hovers beyond the ability of language and thought to fully capture it changes the way we live in the world. All this is partly a factor of age (and, therefore, of experience). It is also partly a factor of intuition.

As one cultivates these qualities, one also begins to accept the imperfectability of life without giving up a notion of ultimate perfection. One's attention shifts from the material world to the transcendent world behind—and beyond—it. As one looks for ways to encounter the presence of the immortal in the limited world of mortality, one becomes less attached to this world.

I find myself beginning this part of the journey. Ideas which would once have seemed absurd to me have taken on an intense relevance. At the same time, I am less absorbed with the daily affairs of the marketplace. Preparing myself to deal with where I am going rather than where I have come from seems not in the least bit strange. Slowly and very tentatively, the exhilaration I feel when I manage even briefly to banish moments-of-death in my life suggests the promise of a future of such exhilaration, and I chase after it.

Are such thoughts unique? Where can people share such thoughts? Where else if not in the synagogue? As a rabbi, I have a somewhat captive audience. My congregation has quite a few older members I assumed would be reticent to consider the implications of their deaths. They seemed so committed to avoiding the subject of mortality that I only reluctantly raised it from the pulpit. Politics and, even, sex, I thought would get a better reception.

I was wrong. While writing these meditations, I also preached many of them. There was some initial discomfort and an occasional complaint. There was confusion and annoyance, especially since some congregants' teachers had assured them that Judaism denied immortality and focused only on this world. There was also heartfelt thanks for legitimizing the subject, and an outpouring of questions, concerns, theories, and experiences. There was a strong desire to address the transcendence of death which had been repressed by a Judaism that had adopted America's taboo on the subject and the modern rationalist taboo about life beyond death.

The most uniquely human affirmation of life is our sense that it does not end with death. I am thankful for the many congregants who have proved to me that this affirmation has not disappeared. I am thankful that I could help some of them discover this affirmation within themselves.

FREE WILL, SAINTS AND DISCIPLESHIP

God chose to create the world as we know it. He created human beings in His image, and endowed us with approximations of His every attribute, including the one which He exercised first—choice. God's first act was to *choose* to create. He was under no compulsion to do so. To be created in God's image implies possessing the divine attribute of Free Choice.

We cannot choose to be immortal. That comes only as a gift from God. Similarly, God cannot choose to die. He cannot become mortal. But people can choose to die. And we can choose to flee God's presence and, by doing so, expand the moments-of-death in life that are caused by God's absence. If we so choose the attributes of love, life-creation, loving kindness, reason, imagination, relationship and sexuality, all can be subjected to a death choice, a choice which turns these attributes on ourselves or on others in ways which are hurtful; thus those attributes that are innately good can become debased.

To some extent, our mortality guarantees this debasement. But the choice of life over death which the Torah lays before us is precisely the choice to celebrate the life-affirming aspects of the divine attributes which we share—to lift them up, rather than to bring them down to the loneliness of death. Yet, too often we humans—precisely because we *are* humans— bring down divine attributes.

The single human attribute of which we are most aware is our mortality, and we respond to it from this acute awareness. Responding more consistently to the attributes we share with God can only come by experiencing them in the lives of others. Jewish tradition, like other religious traditions, has produced some people whose appreciation of their divine attributes inspires others. These people are called saints, *hasidim.* Their lives enhance our sense of the possibility of embracing these attributes since these lives themselves exemplify that potentially holy path.

The saint may have a strong prophetic imagination, or may have been taught by a prophet, or may have been a disciple to a saint or to those who were themselves the disciples of saints. It is in this context that the rabbis said that one should ransom one's teacher before one's father. For one's father brings you to this world, but one's teacher brings you to the world to come.

REPENTANCE

A framework for dealing with the terror of God's absence in death can be found in the normal human emotional response to it—namely, grief. Grief and the process of mourning in the face of death are the models for repentance, which is the normal human emotional response in the face of sin. Repentance begins with anger and denial because we do not wish to acknowledge the terror we experience during moments without God. But to restore God's presence, we must first conquer anger and shame and let ourselves mourn the loss of so many moments-in-life. Our object is not only to mourn, but also, as with the death of a loved one, to allow ourselves to admit the reality of death so that we may be comforted. That comfort, in this case, comes from God's returning to the life of one who has acknowledged his grief and pain at God's absence. This comfort also brings a sense of reconciliation. Re-experiencing God's presence reminds us of our mortality, as well as the redemption which will one day overcome death for us and for all creation.

Thus, we move from grief to mourning, mourning to comfort, comfort to reconciliation with our mortality. Then we move to joy, the joy of our immortal future. This is the fullness of repentance.

ATONEMENT

Atonement is the opposite of exile. It is that moment when we are no longer burdened by the knowledge of our mortality. It is to live, however briefly, as we imagine we would have lived in the Garden of Eden. It is to live in full consciousness of our immortality, and to fully accept the image of the redemption which leads to that immortality. As such, it requires and produces a sense of liberation from death and sin.

To effect such a liberation, we must first become estranged from the moments-of-death in life which have afflicted us. We must also acknowledge our mortality because accepting the inevitability of our own death is a prelude to releasing ourselves from it. Ultimate atonement requires faith that we will eventually be welcomed into a deathless world by an immortal God. An experience of such liberating magnitude must be precipitated by a worship experience of equivalent magnitude. Atonement implies, therefore, the most direct and powerful confrontation with death that we can experience short of death itself.

Every religion has developed rituals which help mortals experience the enormous power of death and taste the liberation which comes with its transcendence. In the prophetic imagination of the Jewish people, this ritual initially focused on the power of sacrifice. In the ritual of sacrifice, we became intimately aware of the death awaiting us, accepted the separation which death imposed between us and God, and then celebrated the release that would follow this death. The flesh-and-blood of the sacrificial animal symbolized our eagerness to be liberated from mortality. But even when the Temple stood and the sacrificial cult flourished, the revelatory tradition of Israel required that the quest for atonement also include a more personal and more intimate "giving up" of our mortality. This was called, then as now, "afflicting the soul," and was understood to include giving over of one's own flesh and blood, through fasting, in liberation from mortality.

Today, when atoning, we still refrain from sexual activity, which is the hallmark of mortality since it symbolizes and assures our physical continuance. We also refrain from washing or adorning ourselves, from clothing ourselves in luxury, from eating or drinking. In this way, we "give up" our concern with our physical nature to achieve the same state of mind that sacrifice once achieved for our people. To these, we add prayer, study, and deeds of loving kindness. If properly done and with the proper degree of attention—and if God is willing—then we have gained atonement.

A separate category of atonement in Jewish tradition is through death itself. Atonement through death is in the hands of God. Since the gulf between this world and the next can only be bridged by God's efforts to remove the barrier of death between them, so also does atonement through death require the intervention of God to provide the passage between life and life-beyond-death which follows the atoning death. Every death atones, and no death is independent of God's intervention in this world. Death cannot be sought outside of God. Such seeking is itself the action of God.

REWARD AND PUNISHMENT

Hope for reward for the good that we do and fear of punishment for our misdeeds is the language in which we express the conflict between life and death in the human soul. Hope for reward embodies our desire to live without sin. Fear of punishment reflects our experience of the inevitable failure of that hope and our acceptance of the fact that such a failure has consequences. Reward and punishment are ancillary to the free will which defines our very mortality. Without reward and punishment, we must posit a world in which the transcendence of mortality is impossible. This would be a world without ultimate reward. Transcendence would not depend on our activities in this world and would be dispensed by an arbitrary God. Both of these possibilities run counter to the experience of God in the imagination of the people Israel.

Some in our tradition fear that human striving to imitate God is somehow debased if performed in anticipation of some kind of reward and punishment. But this misconstrues the Jewish experience of the divine. Logically, God's commandments must have consequences. And nothing indicates that these consequences will not be played out in this world to help us reduce moments-of-death in life, and in the next world so that we can appreciate life without death. To strive to reap the benefits of life without death and to strive to be chastened by punishment are among the highest yearnings available to us.

THE SOUL

The place where God and human beings meet is the imagination. This is where the mortal can sense the presence of the divine and where the divine can make itself known to the mortal. We call that place the human soul.

Hebrew uses two words to describe the soul: *neshama* and *nefesh*. *Neshama* denotes the breath of life that was breathed into the first human by God. It is synonymous with "spirit." *Nefesh* is identified with the life force as it manifests itself in all living creatures. It is metaphorically located in the blood, which is the carrier of life.

The difference between these two terms suggests one of the fundamental religious insights of the Jewish people: that the imagination is as essential to life as the very flow of blood. Accordingly, whatever destroys one's imagination has destroyed life no less than whatever spills one's blood.

The notion of a dual soul—the soul of the flesh and the soul of the spirit—is also integral to our understanding of life, death, and life after death. Since we are both spirit and body, neither is extraneous to our being in this life or the next. Since the definition of our humanity must include our physical and spiritual natures, then the meeting of God and our humanity must include our body and our spirit.

This is the paradox of our nature and it is at the heart of the dual nature of our soul. Together, *neshama* and *nefesh* constitute a paradoxical duality, and a paradoxical duality itself constitutes a unity. *Neshama* and *nefesh* are aspects of the wholeness of ourselves. The two of them equal one soul and the soul unifies our complex being.

PROPHECY

The voice of God as it manifests in the imagination has an existence separate from the imagination, but it is also shaped by the particular imagination which apprehends it. Its apprehension is proportionately imperfect according to the fallibility of humans. Some humans, by virtue of their extraordinary spiritual preparation and/or by the inexplicable gift of God, have transcended the limits of their imagination. These prophets hear the voice of God as it is—outside the particularity of their imagination.

Moses was the greatest of the prophets of the people of Israel. His ability to hear the voice of God as one hears the voice of ones neighbor has not been surpassed. Other prophets and rabbis have also heard the voice of God with an extraordinary clarity. Yet, the absolute authority of these events is mitigated by the fact that God shapes the content of His revelation according to the limits of understanding possessed by those people to whom the prophet must speak.

Prophecy may be attained as a gift of God, but it may also be attained by devoted service to God's Way, the study of the revealed tradition, and the constant excitation of the imagination in order to meet and hear God in it. The methods of such excitation will vary in different traditions. They include meditation, contemplation, study, prayer, and intense engagement with the imaginative works of other teachers.

God may also make His voice appropriately known to prophets from peoples who are not Jewish. Prophecy is God's way of correcting the imperfections of the ongoing traditions of revelation as contained in the oral and written Torah, and in the sacred traditions of other peoples as they proceed through the human imagination. However, the dangers of false prophecy—believing that one has heard the voice of God when one has only heard one's own voice—are such that traditional revelation as developed through the imagination of a people also acts as a correction on prophecy. That which the prophet hears in his or her imagination cannot be radically inconsistent with the revelatory tradition which surrounds it. The embodiment of the revelatory tradition which is both sacred in and of itself and a test of true prophecy, for the people Israel, is *halachah*, the Way of God and People.

SUFFERING

Suffering accompanies life in this world. It is a fact of existence, not an emotional response to it. Therefore, neither sadness nor joy affects the presence of suffering. The source of suffering is our refusal to accept our mortality. Spiritual and physical suffering drives the process of trying to achieve such acceptance. The closer we come to such acceptance, the less we suffer, though our afflictions may be great. The more difficult it is for us to adjust to the inevitable, the more we suffer, though our afflictions may be slight.

But suffering may at least help us recognize moments-of-death in life and the salutary effect of transcending them by drawing closer to God. We then come to realize that just as moments-of-death in life can be transcended, so, too, can death be transcended. Thus, mortality may become less of a disappointment, for it is temporary. No one can help but be disappointed with mortality, but knowledge of a new life can be a balm for this pain. We can learn to welcome the work that suffering helps us do by accepting ourselves—and death— fully, and by expecting to come to life again.

MIRACLES

The many miracles in the Jewish revelatory tradition have often caused discomfort to the heirs of that tradition. In our own times, that discomfort has increased as the scientific view of the world has become more pronounced and more widely accepted. Yet, even in ancient times, the problem of events which seem to defy reason bedeviled a tradition otherwise committed to the sanctity of human reason.

Rightly understood, this should not be so. Miracles are required so that the proper relationship between human reason and our perception of the voice of God might be attained. A miracle, then, is the form of expression best suited for those experiences which defy reason.

Yet the description of a miracle, such as the resurrection of the dead, cannot be understood as expressing a fact that can be established by rational proof. Rather, it must be understood as the form in which the prophet clothes the experience of hearing God's voice in his imagination. He does this in such a way as to allow his audience to experience the same event that he himself experienced. The problem is not solved by proving or verifying miracles, but by the imaginative experience of miracles as a result of a prophet's description of them. At the same time, the language of miracles helps maintain our awareness that while the human endeavor is impossible without reason, it can only be effective in those matters which Koheleth, the author of Ecclesiastes, characterized as being "under the sun." With this phrase, he teaches us that reason has limits beyond which it transforms a gift into a perversion.

Attempting to understand miracles literally rather than seeing them as signposts toward the realities I've been describing reduces them to the level of "fact" which, we assume, can be investigated by reason. Under the scrutiny of such investigation, however, miracles are dismissed and their true power is lost. The loss of the power of miracle invariably diminishes the knowledge of the possibility for gaining victory over death, which is, after all, the ultimate miracle.

TIME AND ETERNITY

The choice of life defines time. Every moment contained in that choice is connected to a past made up of choices made by ourselves and by our ancestors. And every moment contained in that choice immediately makes possible a future circumscribed by a death that, potentially, can be transcended.

Eternity consists only of God. Time is the quality of the sum of all the different forms of the relationship between us and God. Choosing life gives time meaning in this relationship. Choosing death-in-life destroys time. It leaves emptiness as the quality of the relationship between ourselves and God. The Eternal is alone outside of time.

By reminding ourselves of time's meaning, we imbue the passage of time with a nearly constant accumulation of choices for life. Reciting blessings, praying at appointed times, celebrating the Sabbath and festivals at their proper time are all part of our impulse to rescue time from emptiness and to befriend Eternity.

In this way, we gain a past. Jews, in particular, gain the past of Torah and Jewish history and of their family's heritage. We also gain the possibility of a future. Jews, in particular, gain the future of the Messianic world and the salvation of the world to come. And we offer our friendship, to a lonely God. Jews do this by living the life of Torah and *halachah*. Finally, by giving life to time, we prepare ourselves to travel on the path that leads to transcendence and brings time and Eternity together.

6

LIVING IN TWO
WORLDS

The most difficult problem of religious life—and the most difficult problem of all life—is to maintain the appropriate balance between living life only in this world and living a life concerned only with life beyond this world. It is to this conundrum that Jewish experience has responded with such wisdom. By linking every action of life to community and to life beyond materiality the Jew can do the impossible and live in two worlds simultaneously.

Perhaps even more remarkable is that *halachah*'s storehouse of wisdom is available when the questions we ask change as we progress through the various stages of our lives. Moreover, *halachah* prods one not only to ask the important questions, but also to discover the changing questions that one might ask.

As a ten-year-old boy, in love with the synagogue and the shrouded world my grandfather left behind in coming to this country, I had scant idea of the nature of the questions I would eventually bring to my life. As a twenty-five-year-old rabbinic student, I discovered my questions primarily while studying the then-new literature of the Holocaust. Just before boarding my plane from New York for Santa Barbara, where I went, in part, to sort out my relationship with the Judaism I had begun to discover, I purchased Andrew Schwartz-Bart's *Last of the Just.* It was the first book about the Holocaust I'd read and the horror that it evoked combined with the beauty and mystery of the world of European Jewry that it introduced to me began my full return to Jewish life. I would restore in my life the world that Hitler had destroyed. I would remake my grandfather's world in my own image.

As a thirty-year-old rabbi, I had to learn to transfer my commitment to the dead of the past to the dead of the present, from the dead about whom I'd read and who seemed always with me to the dead at whose funerals I officiated. As a thirty-two-year-old bereaved father, I had to somehow assimilate personal tragedy with public tragedy, my private tragedies as a bereaved father and the ongoing effects of the tragedy of the Holocaust as it hung in the air of the Jewish world. And now, at forty-three, I have begun to deal with all the things I will never be able to do and all the people I will never be able to be.

The questions keep coming and the answers keep changing. The impetus to ask them and the resources to attempt to answer them have come from Jewish tradition's Way of God and People, which has allowed me to live in the two worlds of community and spirit.

HALACHAH: THE WAY OF GOD AND PEOPLE

Halachah is prophecy expressed in the details of daily life, the cycles of individual life events and the cycles of natural and national time. It is a living metaphor for the sound of God's voice as perceived by prophets and sages. As such, its content changes over time as different people at different times hear the voice of God and as the tradition of these revelations shape the ongoing revelation.

Halachah is the path which humans and God walk together. It provides the maximum number of moments of eternal life within the confines of mortal existence. It is the attempt to live life as though there were no moments-of-death in life and no sin. Thus, it provides the way for a messiah to accelerate God's intervention into human events so that history might conclude with the cessation of death. The cessation of death removes the ultimate separation between God and us—mortality. It is the goal toward which all of life is directed.

For Jews, *halachah* constitutes the heart of Torah. For other peoples, there are equally binding responses in daily life appropriate to the nature of that people's experience of God's voice. To affirm this bond is to stand poised at the threshold of immortality. To deny it is to live in death.

BLESSINGS: INVOKING THE LIFE MOMENT

Choosing life over death-in-life requires awareness. At every moment, one has such choice and must struggle to attain this awareness. *Halachah* provides the venue for this choice and the opportunity to heighten this awareness. This is the way of blessings. In the blessing, the goal of living life in praise of God, of acknowledging the link between God's immortality and man's mortality, is momentarily achieved.

The grammatical structure of a blessing reveals the paradox of our relationship with God. For example, in a blessing with which most Jews are familiar—"Praised are You, [second person] Lord our God, Ruler of the Universe, He [third person] who causes bread to emerge from the earth"—the God of immortality and transcendence, the God who is wholly different from us is, grammatically, the God of the third person. This grammatical structure emphasizes our distance from God. Yet, this same God has miraculously formed a relationship with us which is personal and can only be expressed in the second person, the grammatical form we use when speaking with a friend.

This paradoxical relationship is manifest in the world around us: in the bread we eat, the flowers of the field, the rituals in which we participate, the movement of the earth through its natural cycles. Therefore, the blessing expressing this relationship embraces both the theological paradox and the natural reflection of this paradox. It is the building block of the liturgy which celebrates these manifestations. By enacting this liturgy, we become cognizant of the gift of life and the possibility of transcending death.

DOING AND HEARING: THE NATURE OF COMMANDMENTS

In the presence of God, we must act. We must *do* even before we *hear.* That is what the people of Israel understood when they responded at Mount Sinai, *"Naaseh V'Nishmah"* ("We will do and we will hear"). Human action is demanded by the commanding presence of God. The content of such action, which is the particular commandments themselves, emerges from the encounter with God in the imagination of the prophet and the sage and is shaped by the imagination and experience of the people they addressed. Therefore, each people will evolve its own particular patterns of response to the commanding presence of God.

The pattern of response itself conveys God's presence and the offspring of the revelation of that Presence. As such, it is a way on which human beings may come, through obedience, to the revelation of that commanding presence to experience something of revelation which their own unaided imagination might not be free enough to otherwise allow. Thus, *"Naaseh V'Nishmah."* Doing leads to hearing. And hearing, of course, leads to strengthening of doing, which, in turn, leads to a more clear hearing. One finally reaches a level of doing and hearing which is akin to prophecy itself.

Not to act in the presence of God is to absent oneself from that Presence. Since God is absent only in the moment of death, we choose death-in-life—sin—when we exclude ourselves from being commanded.

MARRIAGE AND DIVORCE: INTIMACY AND THE DEATH OF INTIMACY

Intimacy is the process in which love, the passionate engagement with another, centers itself in a person's life. Love is not possible in moments-of-death in life. In fact, the disappearance of love is the death of intimacy.

Both the creative impulse of sexuality and the urge to meld our masculine and feminine elements with the passionate engagement of love are active in intimacy. If these urges do not occur within authentic intimacy, they are lust and produce moments-of-death, not moments-of-life.

Marriage is the institution which provides the fullest opportunity for the process of intimacy. Jewish tradition compares marriage to the Temple or Tabernacle in the wilderness: it creates a Jewish home, a *mikdash meot*, or small sanctuary. The dedication of the Tabernacle in the wilderness, according to the Torah, was accompanied by three categories of offerings. The first, a sin offering, and the second, a whole burnt offering, were given entirely to God. The third, an offering to consecrate the new altar, was shared by God and the celebrants.

These three elements are also present in marriage. Every marriage must begin with atonement, which is living, however briefly, as we imagine we would have lived in the Garden of Eden. Thus, in the marriage ceremony we ask God to bless the couple as He did the first man and woman in the Garden of Eden. Every marriage must begin with a recognition of God's ability to love perfectly as compared to our ability to love only imperfectly. And so, we praise God, who created all things for His glory. Every marriage must begin by recognizing the human ability to strive to live in the constant presence of God. This is reflected by praising God who created man and woman in His image so they might perpetuate life.

The wedding ceremony also recognizes that, ultimately, intimacy in the world can only be fully realized in the life of the Messiah. Every marriage potentially presages a return to Zion by the children of Zion since, if intimacy is achieved in one marriage and then in another and in another, the Messianic moment might be precipitated.

Marriage, then, is a microcosm in which individuals learn and perfect the behaviors which produce the conditions for the end of human history as we know it. Such conditions prepare the way for the end of death and for God's entrance into history.

Marriage can also be a microcosm for the affliction of the world by death and by moments-of-death in life. When intimacy fails, when no passionate engagement can transcend the lifelessness that marriage partners see in each other, then the *mikdash meot* is destroyed just as the *Mikdash* in Jerusalem was destroyed by *sinat hinam* (baseless hatred), the enmity between the partners in Jewish society.

Divorce allows mourning for the destroyed *mikdash meot* to proceed. It is the sad but necessary process of recognizing the death of intimacy in our lives, just as mourning for the destroyed Temple allowed Jewish history to proceed. Divorce does not destroy a marriage. The death of intimacy does. Divorce is the recognition of destruction, the beginning of life lived in light of the destruction, the planting of seeds for a possible future *mikdash meot* built on a renewal of intimacy.

KASHRUT: LIFE-GIVING DEATH

The act of eating is quintessentially mortal. The Midrash teaches that angels and human beings in after-life do not eat. This is an eminently logical metaphor because only beings who can—and inevitably will—die need to be concerned with maintaining life. In a world in which moments-of-death in life have been reduced to their minimum in this world, such as in the Garden of Eden, eating is as separated from death as is possible: That is, no blood is shed in pursuit of food. But in the world of exile, in the world filled with potential moments-of-death in life, much blood is shed by humans in pursuit of nourishment.

Ideally, this should be discouraged. When it cannot be avoided, Jews have discovered a system that transforms the inevitable moments-of-death in life associated with eating into moments in which God is made more present.

This system, known as *kashrut*, reduces the weight of death. It operates on three levels. The first is the arbitrary disciplining of the urge to eat by proscribing certain beasts and permitting others. It makes us aware that we are dealing with death and are embarking on a road that separates us from the Divine.

The second prescribes a method for introducing compassion: It injects a moment-of-life into a process otherwise death-filled. By restricting eating flesh torn from a living beast and by forbidding us from eating flesh with its own mother's milk, the Torah provides us with a way to bring some life —and, therefore, something of the presence of God—into the spilling of blood.

Finally, by emulating the method of ritual slaughter used by the priests at the Temple in Jerusalem to slaughter the sacrifices, we try to elevate the act of eating to the life-giving heights of that ritual. We struggle to become aware of our own death and, by sharing it with God, experience the possibility of transcending death.

Thus, an act which begins as an expression of our coarsest mortality helps us move closer to our most sublime potential for immortality.

SHABBAT AND HOLY DAYS: A TASTE OF THE WORLD TO COME

Joy is a foretaste of the world to come. It is a hint of that mode of being in which humans and God are in perfect relationship with one another.

In this life, one can only know joy in relationship with another person. From the wisdom of the Jewish imagination and its revelatory tradition has come practical responses to the necessity of joy in this life in order to sustain our faith in the life beyond death.

Foremost among these responses is the Sabbath, which is the model for prophecy in this world. God and humans draw near to one another in the imagination, where the prophet hears the voice of God and finds the language with which to express what he has heard for others. This is the revelatory tradition.

The Sabbath is the Jewish assertion that these two worlds can become one. On the Sabbath, we are freed from the constraints of worldly cares; we act as though we live in redeemed time. This is a breathtaking act of imaginative daring and, ideally, requires the concerted effort of the entire community of Israel to work. Each Jew who does not participate in this effort removes one layer of imaginative film from the experience of the whole. If enough people do not participate, it becomes impossible for those who do to feel the imaginative actuality of the world-to-come. On the other hand, joining together in an imaginative relationship of all of Israel can be so powerful as to effect not only a taste of the world-to-come, but also its advent.

Shabbat, therefore, provides those who observe it with the faith necessary to pursue the perfection needed to bring redemption by letting them taste its fruits each week. At the same time, it provides the environment for the prophetic experience itself—the experience of imaginative speculation—which is necessary for the pursuit of perfection.

Finally, within each Shabbat is the power to bring on the ideal future whenever humans are collectively ready for it.

May we live to see such perfection in our own time.

SALVATION AND THE WORLD TO COME

In the redeemed world of the Messiah, human beings will be able to realize their highest potential while still embodied. The eradication of death and of its corollary, moments-of-death in life (or sin) will let the body achieve its promised perfection: The support and nurture of the *nefesh* (the soul of the flesh) by the *neshama* (the soul of the spirit).

But beyond the dual soul and beyond the redeemed world of the Messiah, there awaits yet another world. A world not approached by death; a world not only beyond death, but also beyond life. It is the world in which the *nefesh* and *neshama* become One. The body that has been physically resurrected does not die, but will no longer be: the spirit and the flesh that both comprised the body will ascend above the world of creation and the world of redemption to the world of salvation. The lonely God will be eternally united with the subject of His eternal love.

This is the world of salvation for which Jews traditionally pray three times a day. Though we pray each day for a messiah to bring redemption and we understand that in this redeemed time death will have been conquered, we nevertheless continue to pray for the perfection of the body that will ultimately lead to the flourishing of salvation. Only in redeemed time can the body achieve this perfection, which will result in its disappearance. Redemption (which precedes salvation) is a condition for salvation, which is the goal of creation itself.

THE HOLOCAUST: THE WORLD OF DEATH

The world without God is death. The world in which there are only moments-of-death in life is without God. The world of the Holocaust is as close as we have ever come to realizing such a Godless world.

But a world emptied of God is emptied of His image, which is borne by human beings. The Holocaust was a world emptied of God and emptied of human beings. Only the victims and the few who reached out to aid them remained human and, therefore, carried God's presence through the abyss.

A world without God—and consequently without human beings—is a nightmare. It is the return to the chaos that preceded created life. It is the failure of creation. But it is possible. We know that because it has happened.

A world without God is meaningless. But experiencing the possibility of a world without God is also pregnant with meaning. The systematic marginalization of Jews and Judaism from European society—and Jews' acquiescence to this marginalization—had to result in conditions preparatory to the nightmare of a Godless world.

To say that this nightmare has no meaning is to assent to it. Its meaning must be that we have no choice but to choose moments-of-life and the presence of God. Jews and gentiles alike must seek the paths by which they can choose life rather than despair in the face of death. Jewish tradition affords Jews the shape of such paths as they have been cultivated until now. The future articulation of that tradition must continue to be guided by this necessity.

The nightmare must mean that there is an absolute necessity for the existence of the Jewish people and their Torah in the making of this choice for non-Jews also. To reject the Jewish people is to reject the possibility of making a choice for life in every other tradition.

The Holocaust was the price that the world paid for rejecting God and the people of God. Yet its victims were, primarily, that very people. This paradox has been an accusation against God since then. That is, just those people who believed they lived their lives in such a way as to choose moments-of-life in this world, were paid back with death. I reject this accusation. If the choice is to live in a world without God or to die from the absence of God, the Jew has no choice but to die: *that* becomes the choice for life. For those who might have thought that "choosing life" was a mere slogan, the Holocaust is the experience of the seriousness of our quest for life. For those who might have thought that they would not be affected by others' choices against life, the Holocaust is the experience of the inescapability not only of choosing life for ourselves, but also of insisting that our society choose life. God was not absent from the Holocaust. He was present in the terrible choice for life of the victims, having been abandoned by the choice for death of the Nazis.

Chaos gave rise to creation primordially. Chaos gave way to creation again in our time. But the existence of that chaos was shown to be closer than we might previously have dreamed. Thus we cannot afford to dream-any longer. We can only afford to more vigorously affirm life over death, or risk being swallowed by a death whose presence we have tasted in no uncertain terms.

POSTSCRIPTS

REVELATORY
PERSONAL
METHODOLOGICAL

A Revelatory Postscript: Interpreting The Ten Commandments

The Torah is grounded in the experience of revelation at Sinai. By describing those events as the simultaneous hearing of God's voice in the imagination of Moses and in the collective imagination of the people of Israel gathered below him, the Torah articulates the unparalleled uniqueness of this particular revelation. Its content comprises the most fundamental of all such moments. All subsequent revelations occur to extend this revelation.

The *experience* of revelation is what is meant by an unchanging Torah, an experience to which we may neither add nor subtract. The content of this experience certainly changes over time and under the impact of historical circumstances. This revelation functions, imaginatively, as the re-creation of the world or as the renewal of creation after redemption. It describes what human beings must be dedicated to in order to fulfill their role in creation. It also describes the major impediments to that fulfillment which are caused by their very mortality.

I

"I am the Lord your God who brought you out of the land of Egypt, out of the house of bondage." *

The existence of God is inextricably bound up with redemption. From the human perspective, the mystery of God's being is entirely contained in our knowledge of our mortality, our confrontation with death, and His revelation that death will be transcended. The first principle of human knowledge and action is to be constantly mindful of this fact.

*Translation of the Ten Commandments is the author's.

II

"You shall have no other gods beside me. You shall not make for yourselves any carved idol, or any likeness of anything that is in heaven above, or that is in the earth below or that is in the water under the earth; you shall not bow down to them, nor serve them, for I, the Lord your God, am a jealous God, punishing the iniquity of the fathers upon the children unto the third and fourth generation of those that hate me, but showing mercy to thousands of generations of those that love me and keep my commandments."

The logical extension of the first principle of God's being is not to be distracted from it by the world of creation. It is precisely this world which affords us the venue for achieving redemption. To substitute the venue for the goal is idolatry and acceding to idolatry inevitably brings pain and suffering. This punishment emerges from the relationship of parents to children just as the reward for love of God is carried through thousands of generations.

The second principle on which human destiny rests is the avoidance of idolatry. The transgression of this principle works itself out in the relationship of parents to children.

III

"Thou shall not take the name of the Lord in vain; for the Lord will not hold him guiltless that takes His name in vain."

The power which we and God share in shaping the meaning of creation is speech. To take God's name in vain is to represent in speech the same idolatry that is expressed by idol worship. When we deceive ourselves that we are worshipping the True God while actually worshipping ourselves, we take God's name in vain. When we say that we know better than God what the creation means and invoke His Name as justification, we have invoked His Name in vain. For this, the guilt of idolatry will afflict us as much as for outright idol worship.

IV

"Remember the Sabbath day, to keep it holy. Six days shall you labor and do all your work; but the seventh day is a Sabbath to the Lord thy God; in it you shall do no manner of work, you, nor your son nor your daughter, nor your manservant, nor your maidservant, nor your cattle, nor your stranger that is within your gates. For in six days the Lord made heaven and earth, the sea and all that is within them and rested on the seventh day, therefore the Lord blessed the sabbath day and hallowed it."

God's being as redemption and His unity demand that we avoid all possibility of idolatry—in speech, in thought, or in action. The world which we could create by abolishing idolatry completely is the world of order of the Sabbath, the world of redemption wherein a redeemed humanity lives without death.

The Sabbath is a microcosm of the world to come. It helps prepare the way to salvation. By refraining from mastery over creation on the Sabbath, we practice the highest antithesis to idolatry. We submit fully to our proper role in creation and acknowledge that "the earth is the Lord's and the fullness thereof."

V

"Honor your father and your mother that you may live long in the land which the Lord your God is giving to you."

At the very center of the revelatory moment at Sinai is the principle of reconciliation between parents and children. Before this moment, the Torah had already dramatized the centrality to redemption of this relationship in the stories of the struggles between Abraham and Isaac, Isaac and Jacob, and Jacob and his children. After Sinai, prophet after prophet will point to the parent-child relationship as essential for achieving redemption. Their warnings culminate in the prophecy of Malachi, the last of the prophets: "Behold, I will send before you Elijah, the prophet, before the coming of the great and dreadful day of the Lord: And he shall turn the heart of the fathers to the children and the heart of the children to their fathers lest I come and smite the land with a curse."

In one generation's relationship with another, we must acutely confront our own mortality and our desire for immortality. In the growth of our children, we see the transitoriness of our physical selves. We rebel. We futilely play God and attempt to shape our children into ourselves. Rather than encourage them to find God's Presence in their own lives, we often insist that they relive our lives. By doing this, we try to deny our mortality Yet as children, we fled from the mortality of our parents, asserting that somehow we will be different: *we* will live forever. When our parents offer us the wisdom of their mortality, when they attempt to teach us about our helplessness without God in the face of mortality, we reject both.

And so, the misunderstanding of one generation after another is a consequence of our fear of mortality and our delusion of immortality. Only redemption itself, an act of God through the life of the Messiah, can break this cycle of generational misunderstanding. In the Sabbath of redeemed time, death will be conquered and parents and children will turn their hearts toward each other. But the struggle to prepare a world for redemption requires that—in this world, too—parents and children attempt to see beyond their disappointments and delusions regarding one another.

This fifth statement of the fundamental moment of revelation describes the culmination of life after redemption. It is also the first of the statements of warning of the major impediments to redemption itself. It is followed by the other fundamental impediments to redemption.

VI

"You shall not murder."

Murder is the ultimate idolatry. It infuses life with a death that is not accompanied by any sense of transcendence. In murder, humans play God. They determine who shall live and who shall die. Murder drives the possibility of redemption from the world.

VII

"You shall not commit adultery."

Adultery represents putting material desires at the center of one's consciousness. By such an act, the material world, which is otherwise a gift, is perverted. Since we are created in the image and likeness of God, our embodiment is not incidental to our creation. Our bodies are tools for achieving the world to come. The breach of faith of adultery prevents us from even remembering the promise of redemption.

VIII

"You shall not steal."

Similar to murder and adultery, theft attempts to use material power as control over the spirit of a fellow human being. It asserts one's own divinity where this is patently false. It is worship of the self, the most dangerous form of idolatry.

IX

"You shall not testify falsely against your neighbor."

Lying results from our inability to recognize the Divine Presence in our fellow human being. It perverts our most divine-like endowment—speech.

X

"You shall not covet your neighbor's house; you shall not covet your neighbor's wife, nor his servant, male or female, nor his ox, nor his ass, nor anything that belongs to your neighbor."

False testimony, theft, adultery, murder, and our denial of mortality as parents and as children all emerge from our susceptibility to envy. Our inability to allow anyone else to possess more than what we possess (or, sometimes, to possess something different from what we have) is at the root of our estrangement from life's transcendent possibilities.

The enigma of our existence is fully articulated by our record of the encounter between God and humans at Sinai. We are physically and spiritually powerful enough to act the part of God. But, in acting the part of God, we come to worship ourselves. This is the meaning of idolatry. In worshipping ourselves we deny our mortality. We refuse the confrontation with our mortality by means of which we sense our relationship with God. We are consigned to live in the valley of the shadow of death, never to transcend it.

Let us eschew our power of false divinity If we unquestioningly recognize our mortality and its unalterable distance from the immortality of God, then we paradoxically conquer our very mortality. Then, in our inevitable death as mortals, we are able to achieve the immortality which was behind our quest from the beginning.

A PERSONAL POSTSCRIPT

"Why, it has occurred to me to ask myself, do I so frequently choose death, transience and the grave as subjects of my paintings? One must submit oneself many times to death in order to someday attain life everlasting. "

Caspar David Friedrich, Romantic Painter (1774-1840)

So much is still a mystery. Yet, life and death, love and pain, though essentially mysterious, provide the environment for our discovering as much meaning as we are capable of discovering. My journey is not over. Death has not had the final word in my life. On the contrary, my frequent encounters with death have helped enliven each of my days.

Death's gift to me is the experience and understanding that I can learn something about the life of the spirit by analogy with its effect on the life of the flesh. The sensation I sometimes still have of being cut-off, cold, uninviting, I immediately recognize as the onset of yet another death in my life. Recognizing this—and strengthened by my having transcended this type of death before—I am prepared to try again.

Like so many of us, I live in a world where it has become all too easy to let the deadness of spirit that we inevitably feel at one time or another settle in us permanently. Like most families, mine lives at a hectic pace. My wife and I are out of the home all day. We are often distracted in the evening. We have two adolescents and a pre-teen to keep up with. The children's lives are almost as demanding and busy as ours. We are all too often silhouettes passing each other as on a screen.

That, I believe, is what it is like to be dead: to be unable to reach out, to be unable to accept the reaching out of others toward us. It is this death that I still struggle to transcend. I have not triumphed over the anger that comes from living a stressful life. I have not learned how to avoid petty jealousies or feelings of rejection. Nor have I purified my thoughts so that I am never tempted by envy or deceived by pride. However, with the help of Jewish tradition and Jewish practice, with the help of God and with the unstinting love that binds me to so many people, I sometimes can transcend these moments-of-death in my life. When, even in the midst of one of these moments, I turn to the prayerbook to recite the afternoon service, the music that has been with me since childhood again transports me to the world of transcendence. When, in the midst of my hectic day, I am forced to cease my activities and focus my attention on the rituals of the Sabbath or Festivals, I can be transported to the world of transcendence. When, in the throes of some personal pique, I turn and open myself to the love of my family, I feel the love of God and am transported to the world of transcendence.

Many traditional books of Jewish moral instruction begin with a disclaimer about their originality I will conclude with a similar disclaimer. What I have written is not new. But, burdened by the hectic pace of life, it is easily forgotten. The power to recognize death in our lives, to transcend it, and to ultimately gain immortal life, is always in our hands. God has given that much to us. I have extended a reminder, an invitation: We can live more fully by choosing the path of life.

A METHODOLOGICAL POSTSCRIPT

Some further explanation is required concerning this work. The very subtitle that I have chosen for it is something of a paradox, at best, and misleading, at worst. What is a theological meditation? What is theology? It is the way in which human beings reason toward an awareness of God. It is not philosophy. Philosophy is the way in which human beings reason toward Truth, which may or may not turn out to be God.

What, then, is the purpose of theology? It is to bring about the disappearance of theology. This may sound very similar to Ludwig Wittgenstein's proposal for the purpose of philosophy. This is not accidental since Wittgenstein's concern was to show what language could and could not express and to limit philosophy to analyzing what language could legitimately express. Language must make sense. It does this through the application of logic to words, which is grammar. However, Wittgenstein stressed, what can be expressed logically in language does not exhaust the range of human experiences in need of expression. As he wrote in *Philosophic Investigations*, "To say 'This combination of words makes no sense' excludes it from the sphere of language and thereby the domain of language. But when one draws a boundary it may be for various kinds of reason … [boundaries between science, metaphysics and religion, for example]; and so on. So if I draw a boundary line that is not yet to say what I am drawing it for." Language must make sense, but experience comprises both sense and what I will call, knowing full well the danger of misunderstanding that I risk, non-sense.

Expressing the fullness of experience, sense and non-sense, is the world of the sacred. The sacred is part of nature. It is not illogical, but meta-logical. It requires a different mode of seeking than the purely philosophical. It requires the imposition of non-sense rules, of what we might call anti-logic. In language, such an imposition of rules results in Poetry, whether in verse or in prose.

"Poetry proper is never merely a higher mode of everyday language," wrote Martin Heidegger. "It is rather the reverse: Everyday language is a forgotten and therefore used-up poem, from which there hardly resounds a call any longer."

In the everyday world, we treat language as though it were univocal: when we understand its meaning, it is used up. That is, we are not prepared to hear meanings behind the surface meanings of words. In the world of the sacred, we approach language confident that it is open-ended, that it must mean not only what it seems to say but also everything it could possibly say. This Poetry of Being is expressed in every modality, not only in language. The Poetry of movement is Dance; the Poetry of voice is Song; the Poetry of color is Painting; the Poetry of form is Sculpture. All of these constitute the world of nonsense which, from time immemorial, has been understood as the sacred.

I call the natural functioning of these ways of sacred expression "imaginative theology" in order to distinguish it from what theologians do. That I call "discursive theology." When one attempts to replace imaginative theology with discursive theology by trying to express in normal language what can only be expressed in sacred language, one is doomed to fail. Worse, one distances people further from God. But the tendency in certain historical periods to apply the rules of ordinary language to sacred language, and to take it literally, breeds surprise and dismay when sacred language taken this way appears as non-sense. The proper goal of discursive theology is to become imaginative theology and to check the error of those who read sacred language as ordinary language. It can ultimately become imaginative theology and return theology to Poetry.

Meditation functions in this sense as a poem in prose. It is language which must stretch itself in order to express both the sense and non-sense of the world. Theological meditation is something of the middle ground between discursive theology and imaginative theology. The former continues to have a job to do in our confused culture. It explains to people how to read with new rules, dance with new steps, sing with new melodies. The creation of a genuine imaginative theology can only occur when this task has been accomplished. My contribution, such as it is, is to point toward a regeneration of that natural imaginative process which creates sacred language out of the experience of sense and non-sense elements in the world.

ABOUT JEWISH LIGHTS

People of all faiths and backgrounds yearn for books that attract, engage, educate, and spiritually inspire.

Our principal goal is to stimulate thought and help all people learn about who the Jewish People are, where they come from, and what the future can be made to hold. While people of our diverse Jewish heritage are the primary audience, our books speak to people in the Christian world as well and will broaden their understanding of Judaism and the roots of their own faith.

We bring to you authors who are at the forefront of spiritual thought and experience. While each has something different to say, they all say it in a voice that you can hear.

Our books are designed to welcome you and then to engage, stimulate, and inspire. We judge our success not only by whether or not our books are beautiful and commercially successful, but by whether or not they make a difference in your life.

For your information and convenience, at the back of this book we have provided a list of other Jewish Lights books you might find interesting and useful. They cover all the categories of your life:

Bar / Bat Mitzvah • Bible Study / Midrash • Children's Books • Congregation Resources • Current Events / History • Ecology / Environment • Fiction: Mystery, Science Fiction • Grief / Healing • Holidays / Holy Days • Inspiration • Kabbalah / Mysticism / Enneagram • Life Cycle • Meditation • Men's Interest • Parenting • Prayer / Ritual / Sacred Practice • Social Justice • Spirituality • Theology / Philosophy • Travel • Twelve Steps • Women's Interest

About the Author

Ira F. Stone, rabbi of Temple Beth Zion-Beth Israel in Phildelphia is a teacher of theology at The Jewish Theological Seminary of America.

Printed in the USA
CPSIA information can be obtained
at www.ICGtesting.com
JSHW012041140824
68134JS00033B/3201

9 781683 362845